A Few Words for January

For Moe—
I hope you enjoy
these words!
— Sheely L. Feedche
Oct. 1998

A Few Words for January

Shelley A. Leedahl

Thistledown Press Ltd.

Canadian Cataloguing in Publication Data
Leedahl, Shelley A. (Shelley Ann), 1963 –
A few words for January

Poems.
ISBN 1-895449-69-3
I. Title.

PS8573.E3536F48 1997   C811'.54   C97-920003-2
PR9199.3.L394F48

Book design by A.M. Forrie
Typeset in 11 pt. Goudy by Thistledown Press Ltd.
Printed and bound in Canada by
Veilleux Impression à Demande Inc.
Boucherville, Quebec

Cover painting
Christiane Pflug
Canadian, 1936-1972
Kitchen Door with Ursula, 1966
oil on canvas
164.8 X 193.2 cm
Collection of the Winnipeg Art Gallery; Purchased with the
assistance of The Women's Committee and The Winnipeg
Foundation (Accession #: G-66-89)

Thistledown Press
633 Main Street
Saskatoon, Saskatchewan
S7H 0J8

Thistledown Press acknowledges the support received for its
publishing program from the Saskatchewan Arts Board and
the Canada Council Block Grant program.

For the children

CONTENTS

We'd sneak Jimmy in through the back door
and lead him to the cellar
while Mother was busy with sewing or dusting,
ironing Dad's white shirts for work.

We took Jimmy down to the dark rooms
with earthen walls, past the old bathtub,
the wringer washer, into the cold room
where Mother never went
and our broken beer bottles
littered the floor.

Jimmy took off his socks and shoes
and walked across the shards
for a nickel, a dime, whatever
he was offered and we could find
in our mother's jacket pockets.

All that Indian summer,
Jimmy walked on glass
and we were amazed until the one day
Mother called us upstairs
and we had to sneak Jimmy back out
on his razor-sharp feet.
And we would have gotten away with it
except for the tiny bloodprints
he left across Mother's
newly-washed floor.

i.

In grade one
our chances of catching lice
were just a little better
than the odds
of getting scabies

most of us had both

the girls soon learned
wearing a dress
to school
was dangerous
hard to tell your mother
though
(all those pretty new school dresses)
even a teacher's presence
would not stop
the boys
from crawling
under your desk
for a grope
she was too old
to teach anyway
the day she fell
and her varicose veins burst —
kids laughed

hometime was any girl's nightmare
not sure why those
older boys
chased you
but knew
you'd sooner die
than be caught

and you ran

ii.

In the spring
a classmate went missing
a quiet boy
not a troublemaker
like some
of the others
cops found him
in a field   dead
from a gunshot
they think it was an uncle

school is supposed to be fun

I only remember the running

When I think of them I think of the night. The doorbell.
Mother's soft voice. Me waking to find two new brothers.

It was always like that. Cops, social workers and more kids on
the doorstep. *Priscilla's going to stay with us for awhile. Let's make
up a bed for Brad.* Bawling newborns. Reticent two-year-olds.
The teens never stayed very long. I thought we had the biggest
family in the world.

The two kids in this picture, squinting out sun. I've long since
lost their names. I heard the older one shot his head off in
Edmonton. The other one just disappeared.

When my father snores
in the room next to mine,
it could be ten demons
from the dark depths of Hell,
someone trying to talk
with his tongue torn out,
the voice of a dying dog.
It could be the sound
of thirty rats eating,
forty bats beating,
or a young child·locked
in a small black box,
but no, it is only father,
snoring.

for my brothers and sisters

Each December we received it, free
from the local Co-op.
We flipped through it quickly
at first, found our birthdays,
always a weekday,
judged the photograph
that represented our month
and learned which province
had been chosen to salute us.

*If you could be in any one of these pictures
right now, which one would you choose?*
I always chose the ocean

We checked for holidays, anniversaries, full moons.
Scribbled appointments in pencil crayon
    Brownies at 7:30
    hockey practice Sunday.

Young dreamers.
We expected golden chrysanthemums in April,
fields of poppies in June.
December, you betrayed us
with your promise
of laughing faces, hay rides,
warm winter sun.

Later we severed the months
from their pictures,
created colourful fans
or weaved placemats.

Saskatchewan
always had elevators.

When summer spreads her bare brown legs
all the town kids beat it to the lake
in fast cars they'll have totalled off
by the end of the season.

You've gotta grab the few hot ones
and settle down on the beach
with a babe, a beer and some summertime tunes.

This ain't no California, but you can't tell
them that.   These kids forget
this is the north when summer spreads
and they're riding the heat waves,
and if you squint just right, even you will believe
those giant evergreens are palm trees.

for Darb

I remember us, so much alike,
so much in love with tough guys
who drove muscle cars and smoked
too much dope. It's easy
to look back, recall faces
brightened by fires at bush parties,
weekends at the lake, the warmth
of our lovers' bare skin.
We were too young to have felt such heat.

I saw your boyfriend slam his fists in your face.
Blood streamed from your nose, through your fingers.
My boyfriend hit me only once, he burned me
without leaving scars.

After high school, you and I grew apart.
If there were letters, I don't remember.
Still, there's one night that binds us.
It was nearly Christmas. We were driving
to your house on the edge of town.
I still feel the swell of the car,
the heave as we drove over the drunk.
Then us running past the body,
eyes burning in the cold,
our shoes sliding down the icy highway
to the first lighted house.

I wasn't supposed to know. *Just some crazy drunk*, my father
said, slamming down the phone. I knew it was something
about me, whatever terrible thing he'd heard to make his face
turn the colour of newsprint and his legs buckle beneath him, I
knew it must have been about me.

Like the time my older sister wanted to tell me what Grandma
said just before she died and I covered my ears and screamed
No, No, No, so I wouldn't be able to hear. I knew
Grandma had said something about me.

After Dad went to bed, I talked Mom into telling me.
She didn't want to, but I could con her into anything.
Once I made her say *I hate you,* just because I felt like hearing
those words come out of her mouth.

Now I wish I could put my hands over my ears and scream and
pretend I never heard her tonight, but I'm too old for that.
We've got your daughter's legs spread from here to Glaslyn. I wish
I didn't know they meant me.

It was such a cold winter, 1985.
We scraped circles off the crystallized dance
on our windows, saw plump white ghosts
sitting in trees across the lane.

It was a beautiful, slow time. A snowed-in time.
I told your father we should name you January,
after the quiet perfection of snow.
No, he said, *you cannot name the child after cold*.

That frozen morning in the third month,
I took a number in the hospital's admissions.
Sat quietly through the feverish child,
the glue-intoxicated woman.
Kept my knees clamped, holding you in.

Your grandmother prayed, said it would be all right.
I could not forgive them, Mother or God,
for a long time, for letting me hope.

It was such a cold winter.
After they took you.
I thought only of replacing
what I had lost; the emptiness
no one would speak of.

This poem is for you, my mysterious one,
cradled warm in my womb for three solid months.
Sleep sweetly, snow angel, with the prettiest,
the coldest name.

As a child, there was always water
in my dreams. Oceans' great waves, rivers
and the cold northern lakes I knew best.
Dreams of surfing, fishing, diving off cliffs.

I wonder if this was because at age two,
I was rescued from drowning, yet never afraid,
always wanting to be one
with the water. Or perhaps oceans
are what all prairie children dream of.

Now, I sleep on a waterbed; imagine
I'm floating on waves pushed by warm breezes
in the middle of this dry prairie city.

Now, I leave dreaming to my daughter.
She, too, has no fear of water — jumps in
where it is deepest, lets the cold wash over her
thin chest, pale shoulders, silken hair. She calms
me with her sleeping; I put my ear to hers,
listen to sounds of the ocean.

From my kitchen window
the season is orderly, predictable.
Water floods the black garden,
kids stomp in the luscious earth,
jump from the few icy islands
to where water swells
over rubber boot tops.

I will let them play;
chance pneumonia, long hours of laundry
to see their mud-splashed faces.
They dump pailfuls of water,
and watch the new puddles,
squeeze the dark soil
through their fingers.

Who am I to tell them:
Come out of the garden,
and risk destroying everything
growing and glorious.

Here on this country road,
trudging into snowfilled ditches,
we gather the precious willows.

Logan's hand in mine,
small and warm
like the burning white spot
high above us this April morning.

Look, there's some.

He points to a cluster
of budding pussy willows.
I break off the red branch,
add it to our sober bouquet
of brome grass and hawksbeard.

We are discovering together:
two geese, rabbit tracks,
a perfect bird's nest.
Logan ahead of me, running
mud to snow, road to ditch.
He stops, tilts his blonde head:

Listen. You can hear the snow melt.

Taylor and I, crosslegged on the rug
before the full-length mirror,
me pulling the comb
through her straight wet hair
to gather and bind it,
high on her head.

The comb changes hands,
we change positions.
My daughter stands behind me,
gently slides the comb down,
down, until she is kneeling,
must rise again to repeat the strokes.
There is nothing to clutter this
perfect, simple exchange.

I love to watch
your large, workman's hands
fumble with the tiny buckles
on our daughter's best white shoes.
Her thin ankle,
so safe and lovely
in your gentle, callused grip.

i.

This is not an April shower.
The month is October, the rain torrential.
Umbrellas bloom like flowers
in fast-motion: magenta, amarillo and black.

Rain flattens wheat fields,
floods our basement. My daughter sings
rainy day songs.

Rain, rain, go away.

ii.

In red rubber boots,
my son splashes outside.
One, two, three, four, he saves earthworms
from certain drowning.
He shows me the collection,
a slow writhing of flesh tones.

It's raining, it's pouring,
the old man is snoring.
I have thirty-four dead worms
in my kitchen.

iii.

Here comes the rain again,
falling on my head like a memory.

This one is my song.
When I was a child, I'd catch rain
on my tongue, wash my hair in the rain barrel
water. In my room the soft patter
would lull me to sleep.
Even my dreams were greener.

iv.

I tell my kids about Noah.
Noah knew about rain.
Rain rain, go away.
About rain before rainbows.
It's raining, it's pouring.
I imagine his wife, like me,
sat beside windows and listened
to the rhythms.

It's like that first step
once the training wheels go.
His father and I both there
on the street, me running ahead
to preserve the blessed event
with my ever-ready camera,
his father steadying him,
then letting go.

I never thought we'd reach this
day of independence. Now speed's
his best and newest friend.
I always thought something terrible
would take him from us,
crib death or molesters,
or I'd lose him while shopping,
momentarily forgetting I was a mother
because I was so young
and sometimes it was easier
to forget.

But now he's five and riding,
his eager legs fast and strong
on the red birthday bike,
the wind in his ears and me
loving him hard, feeling the wind,
learning to let him go.

We feel adventurous,
wade into the river crowd
of babies and grandmas,
lovers and music.
We and our preschoolers,
way past bedtime,
wide eyes focused
on a bright light,
waiting.

Stars
colour our sky,
the pink especially brilliant.
Fast-falling yellow
is the straight long strands
of Rapunzel's golden hair.
Sea urchins
puffed in green and orange,
vivid against their black sea.

In the finale
we are treated
to a spectacular new design —
high-tech fireworks
in our son's eyes.

It's a miracle it happens at all,
but somewhere between Ben's shitty pants
and *Disney's Duck Tales*,
I start to feel the need,
but I *need* to find a paper
before the words leak out
and are lost because someone's
biting the baby,
the fish are floating upside down,
no one's seen Missy for an hour
and *I want some juice!*
in five-part harmony
pushes all thoughts of paper and poems
back into the river of grey
where it's so hard
to fish them out.

Some days I do cartwheels
just because that's the kind of day
I'm having.
My head's spinning
so I think my body should too.

Most times I lock doors,
close blinds,
but some days I forget
and neighbours catch me:

*Look at the crazy woman.
And they let her have children?*

But they'll never stop me
from flipping, wheeling,
legs in the air,
chasing my thoughts
all over the place.

for Heather

I'm four days trapped inside my home
with two kids, waiting for city snow crews
to reach my street; cabin fever
is setting in. This white isolation
makes me think of you, Sister. Miles away
inside that maze of country roads,
you and your small son in the trailer.

If I called you right now,
we'd talk about our children's sore throats
and cars that won't start, neither of us
wanting to hang up the phone and let go
of each other's voice. But we never speak
of winter's silence and solitude.
It's loneliness, not cold, that threatens.

Four days and I'm reeling; lock myself
in the bathroom while my kids pound
on the door.

How do you do it, sister? Where do you go?
You, who know so much better than I
about winter and isolation.

Today I imagine snow drifting around your farm
like a frothing white sea. You hang on tight.
You roll with the waves.

You'd think it was the moon
I was going to, not just a writers' colony
a few hours away.
Who will take care of the kids?
How will they get along without you?
And, the one I hate the most:
Have a good holiday.

One writer friend said she made a list
for her husband, detailing all the things
he must do for the kids each day.

And there's this man here,
he has to phone his wife every night.

What has happened to this world
where people can't be themselves
because they are always someone's mother,
or husband or wife?

What would people say if they knew
some days I just sit
at my computer and let my fingers
dance over the keys
in no particular order, just because
I like the way it sounds?

Or the hours I spend standing
at the windows, looking at the lake
and snow and everything is perfect
just because it's there
and quiet and not calling me,
not asking or demanding
a goddamn thing.

Jenny sleeps with angels, her mother tells me,
and leaves the young girl in my care

I watch her closely for signs of Divinity, careful
not to hurt the black woollen hair as I work it

into some order, then send her, yellow knapsack bouncing,
to her lessons at the nearby school

Jenny prays before eating, unlike the other children
who gather at my table for lunch

Dear Jesus, hear my prayer   I pray that Mommy
gets money so we can buy some bread

After, she thanks me with feathery kisses
and sings, *Jesus Loves Me*, in Spanish

When we are alone, I ask about angels
What is it like when they're asleep on her sheets,

white, shining, beside her   Jenny won't talk
about sleeping with angels, but her prayers
have small wings of their own

Blanca trusts me with her children
while she learns English downtown
but it's months
before she speaks of Manuel.

When she fled Guatemala
she left behind everything
It was night   Manuel was asleep

I ask how old this son was when she left
Silence rides up like a storm   flies her
out of my kitchen through a jungle
of memory   to a darkness
I have never known

Does she remember the shape of his face
the warmth of his skin   his little boy's voice
calling Mamá?

Blanca sips coffee   black as her long braid
Eyes like the moons on that eve of escape

I think he was seven   she says

I have no business telling you about Lisa.

She was two. The kind of kid you always smile at but never get to know. Five winters ago, I met Lisa and her mother, Marie in our apartment building. The one where I once saw a rat climb the stucco right outside my window.

Marie stopped me in the hall, asked if I'd join her for tea.

Sometimes women have to tell you their secrets; I know about things like that.

I didn't want to hear about her ex-husband, how he spread vaseline on their bed then pissed all over it, but I listened.

All that tranquil afternoon, we sipped tea like perfect ladies while Marie told me how she found out about Lisa.

It was bathtime. It was the way Lisa touched the soft folds of her young body.

But daddy does it.

Sometimes, when it's real bad, you just gotta tell someone, and now I'm telling you. How can I forget that afternoon of tea and tender mercies, the man who touched his small daughter there and there?

Years after, she continues to see his
powerful shoulders, tight-muscled thighs in the bodies
of other men. On streetcorners, in bus stations —
always, they are walking away.

Sometimes, it's the field-fresh smell
of him. A glimpse of the dark windswept hair,
the way it shaded his eyes the last time
they spoke. Once, at a party, she heard his laughter.
How it sounded those first years
when nothing could touch them,
before anyone dared even try.

She sleeps with detailed dreams of him
and his smiling lover. Their faces locked perfect in time.
Her daughter finds pictures, asks: *Who is this man?*
Where is her Daddy standing?

She will warn her daughter about the dangers
of asking questions: *Do you still love me?*
Don't you care how I feel? Is there a chance?

It is a slow death each time she remembers
the moonbright night, waiting
for what would fall from his lips.
Three small stones: *no, no, no.*

Whenever I see a beer commercial,
I think of you. You're one of those
football throwing kinda guys
who thrives in the wind,
sun and laughter of male friends.
Real friends. Beautiful women
are also in the picture.

At your age I had two children
and feet that had long since stopped dancing
with men like you.

I wonder how you see me. Safe
in my life with a husband, a circle
of friends who would bore you.
I bore you, too. You say
I worry too much about money
and the habitual order of things.

But don't write me off yet.
I'm not one of those flawless TV models
who pass out the frosted beer; their pleasure
only lasts thirty seconds. It would shake you
to know the places I've been
and things I have done.
What I could return to,
anytime.

You are only two years younger than me,
but age has nothing to do with it.
You'll celebrate thirty, embrace forty, then fifty.
Laughing, loving, living
your beer commercial life.

(Eavesdropping At The Unemployment Office)

here we are   back at Manpower   what no welcome mat? /geez
the lineup is depressing   what number are you?   I'm 73 they
just called 16 / it's 10:30 / the bum in the green pants and wide
tie   he'll never get a job   probably doesn't want one / look at
that poor broad   kids are giving her fits   bet she got knocked
up   quit school   old man took off   tough luck / the kid in the
Levi 501's might be lucky   young enough   should have
swallowed the gum though / finally   same questions   can't
you look at me lady? / yah   I know   the job postings / what
the hell   may as well check   this is always a real ego booster /
let's see   calculus tutor   naw too easy / banjo instructor   waste
of my talents / no-run pantyhose distributor   I'm sure   what is
this   a joke? / ha   social worker in buffalo narrows   shit
they'd have to give me danger pay for that / hmmm   physical
therapist   nope   overqualified / hey   what's this? / okay guy
move over   let someone else see /

Person required to work on dairy farm.   Previous experience
preferred but will train.

maybe   I milked a cow once / hey   where's all the pencils in
this place? /

It's one week before your staff Christmas party,
the first time I'll meet your new friends
and you watch me now. You want to know
what I'll wear and ask if my black mini-skirt
still fits. I'm tired of tripping over the scale
you place in the bathroom doorway, the magazines
you leave open on skinny-centerfold pages,
the fitness ads you've taped to the fridge.

I just want to tell you, honey, there were seven
cookies in the cookie jar with my name on them
and I ate them all. Slowly. One by one, they melted
on my tongue and I thought of you as I savoured
each sweet chocolate chip.

Twice I have been awakened by poems
beating their tiny fists
inside the cage of my skull
and now this, the smell of egg rolls
drifting down to my bed from the kitchen
where he is slicing and stirring
the ginger and meat.   His nude body
bending over the wok, the quiet muscles
in his arms as he adds wine
and bean sprouts, his tanned thighs
as he walks across the floor.
I ache for sleep yet I conjure his hands,
feel them unpeel me; another poem
coming on.

So far to go and so little time.
The white page, an abyss.
Who can understand this?

Job, maybe,
and Paul
with his mystery affliction.

But I need you to believe
there is also grace
in the wilderness.

I wonder how God felt,
making something out of nothing.

White is the darkest of colours.

Our mothers are moving
in and out of marriages,
apartments, always searching
for cheaper accommodation
and better love.

Tonight we're in a basement,
still waiting for the landlord
who'd promised new paint.
We bought Kentucky Fried Chicken
with beer bottle empties
and spread it out
on a large piece of cardboard.

They want me to ask the blessing.

I know it sounds crazy
but I keep thinking this meal
might be the last supper.
Something big's going to happen
if we can get through this,
something good must be nearby.

I'm not predicting a second coming
or a miracle, but we need a sign,
our poor mothers
need those greener pastures
David spoke of; where are those
still waters, that overflowing cup?

I don't know why they always want me
to ask the blessing.   We're beggars,
we all pray the same thing:

God bless this house; resurrect us.

She didn't want to do it but they'd been out of milk for a week
already and the kids needed new boots and the power
company was threatening and the school wanted money for a
lost book and she had to buy medicine for the youngest and
wouldn't it be nice just to wear a new coat that no one else
had already worn

She didn't want to do it but her husband couldn't keep a job
and she'd never been to school and didn't have any skills and
her children needed her at home and she'd only do it once and
no one would ever have to know

She didn't want to do it but there was this man with the nice
smile who'd helped her pay for the groceries and she couldn't
just let him pity her like that

She didn't want to do it but it wasn't so bad after it was over
and he held her for a minute before he gave her the money
and told her about some of his friends

She didn't want to do it but most of them were just ordinary
men and there was only the one who'd hurt her and even then
he'd paid her extra and she couldn't stop now because the rent
just went up and her oldest boy needs glasses and it's nice to
have fresh fruit and some mothers just love too much

SOMEDAYS ALL I WANT FROM LIFE
IS A PEANUT BUTTER AND BANANA SANDWICH

The mailman brings another rejection —
the local journal which always buys
my stories and poems, no matter
how bad. My husband receives a letter
from Unemployment Insurance, stating
we owe them $912 for an overpayment
they gave us, their mistake.

Yesterday we sold the kids' skates
for $25 and finally had milk
for breakfast. Two days earlier
it had been a joke. I said:
Troy, we have to buy milk,
and he said: *Can't they just have toast*
for breakfast? then realized
we didn't have any bread.
We laughed and laughed.

I wonder how long friends will continue
to see me, considering how often I evade
their requests to go shopping, see shows,
do lunch. I broke down and told one of them:
        We never go for lunch.
        We don't have the money.
I told her how far beneath the poverty line
we live and she wouldn't look at me
but began crying her own blues,
the mortgage payments of two homes,
something I know nothing, will never
know anything about.

Today all I want from life is a peanut butter
and banana sandwich, but the bread's
for the kids and bananas are expensive.
Today even that's out of reach.

My first tornado was like my first man
only better, and I didn't bleed.
Just like that first love,
his tiny photo worn from my eyes
and clipped to fit inside my wallet,
I've captured my first tornado
in a colour glossy and I wield it
at coffee, at parties, show everyone
the dark swirl of it, the tail
sweeping down behind the houses,
just like my first man,
only this lasted much, much longer.

I've been dreaming tornadoes
and I watch the sky,
scoot the kids in at the first sign
of bruised clouds, bawling winds.

My husband doesn't believe the tornadoes
are coming. He laughs when I warn,
store food in the dark space
beneath the stairs. He's blind
to the fury as it gathers
height and speed and spins
violently closer.

I've been dreaming tornados
and making mental lists:
food, water, blankets. It can happen
so fast. In last night's sleep,
we watched the sky shift to black
from our living room window;
the massive cone twisted toward us.
My husband stood stirring
a pitcher of juice
while I lunged to wake the kids,
hide them beneath the trembling stairs.

He just stood there, stirring.

I'm no longer surprised
by uprooted trees,
crushed grain bins and roof tops
in the paths I've recently walked.

I'm learning to calculate
how long it will take, how far
I can go before the sky drops;
tornadoes are never a surprise.

Surprise is discovering a new colour
in a child's eyes, finding a lost lake
in the forest I call home,
or the best surprise yet,
meeting the man I'd never seen
but have always known. How strange
and wonderful to touch his warm skin,
to learn he's both real and beautiful.

I wish I didn't have to warn him
about the cold wind and dark clouds,
how dangerous a tempest can be.

SCARS

It must have been Saturday
for her to crawl back in bed,
leaving water to boil on the stove.
The little girl in her nightie
woke up too early,
pattered into the kitchen —
her tiny hand reached.
The woman ran to the screaming,
swept her from the burning pool,
tore away the soaked nightie,
pulled all the skin off my arms.

Runners, real runners,
do it when no one is watching.
That back alley blast
in the night's darkest hours,
last leap for the nightmare steps.

Necessary running.

Not ladylike, motherly,
not the kind of thing you'd expect
from someone like me, but I am far
from alone.

One woman friend claimed
she was going to run herself to death
and I said: yes,
I know what you mean,
it would be a fine way to go.

Bloodied from recent use,
you clean-cut men
into thin red strips
with your wagging.

              Only I am safe
from this weapon
so easily concealed,
for I am the chosen
who licks clean the blood
from the corners
of your ragged mouth.

The blade is warm
in my mouth,
I cannot feel the barbs,
but there is always the taste
of red death.

All these years you have used it
and still no sign
of the blade beginning to dull.

Yours is the self-
sharpening kind.

I have long wanted to swim with alligators.
Feel their reptilian closeness; my skin
next to scales. See through their eyes
in the swamp's brackish water
where Cooters and Moccasins swim.
At the mercy of climate, gators can't stand the cold.

I, too, cannot tolerate cold.
Ah, but to live in the tropics, like alligators,
close eyes to the sun, refresh with a swim.
Then rest on the sand, brown my skin
perfect copper: the colour of water
at Florida sunset, shade of their alligator eyes.

At dawn, clever gators behind waterweeds eye,
forest mammals at swamp's semi-cold
edge. With crocodilian sureness, water-
dragons attack. SNAP, go their alligator
jaws. Raccoons, muskrats, yet my skin
would be safe; let me climb on their backs, let me swim.

We were both born to swim,
love the lightness of water, their eyes
and that black slit of pupil. I'd skin
the hides from their cold-
blooded hunts, share their alligator
meals, underwater.

It'll be different, at first, other water-
creatures will wonder, but gators will teach me their swim,
how to breed in the water, lay alligator
eggs on the land. How I'll cry when the eyes
of first gators open; the cold
slickness as they dance on my skin.

Hunted by poachers for the soft belly skin,
I'll hide with gators as my flesh turns water-
cool-colours. Scales will come later, as cold
pushes us deeper, we'll swim
to holes, away from all eyes.
More than crocodiles, or gavials, it is alligators

I love best. Alligators of the broad snout, eyes
like biggest marbles, the cold kiss underwater,
plated skin, final grin as I'm welcomed to swim.

she'd always wanted a barbecue so when she finally
got the damn thing she had a party but forgot about the
propane and the sky was all stars and the night was
so warm and the people all left except Joe who was
cool and tossed his smoke into the barbecue and they
lost half the deck and she almost lost Joe and everyone
always said what a hot date she was

There is another world where the air
is perfume and the sun spins
gold on the sea

A boy is lightning across hot sand
bolting   to be at your service
He'll shake each grain of sand from your towel,
smooth out the hills with his boy's black hand

He's quick with *cerveza* and fast with a smile
when he poses for pictures with white girls he knows
could never survive here without him

Pedro I watched you earn pesos today
go home now
your *madre* is waiting

And the buffet is Mexicano.   We are joined by sunburned Canadians who must take the morning plane back to work, worry and two feet of snow in Toronto.

Perhaps they are bitter. Perhaps that's why they tell us about the British solider. He was only eighteen, but he was alone in the city and it was dark. He didn't speak the language, couldn't understand that the cop was asking for money. He should not have walked away.

Now they must wait, all those other British boys on this tropical vacation. Wait for the investigation, the preparation of the body, their cruise ship, a ghost in the harbour.

Back in my room, I go over the Spanish I have studied for months. Not the airport words, the restaurant phrases, but the real words, the ones I might need.

No tengo dinero. I don't have any money. *Puede ayudarme, por favor?* Can you help me, please?

This is my first night.

My husband is a natural in this country. *He* can talk baseball; George Bell, Tony Fernandez, Nelson Liriano. Troy came prepared with Blue Jays cap and T-shirt, things he would have traded — nobody cares.

They want his shoes. White leather running shoes. Troy is 6'2" and towers over the eight or ten Dominicans who surround him. They are staring at his size twelve feet. They want his shoes. *Six T-shirts and five sunglasses,* one of them offers. *Three T-shirts and a conch shell,* yells another. *I give you thirty pesos,* tries a third.

My husband is smiling. He enjoys this. I am suffocating. *Hey lady, wanna buy a T-shirt? You lika these earrings? Flowers, flowers,* says a dry-faced witch. Another woman says nothing, just holds up her palm while the babe in her arm squirms at her breast.

I address them in Spanish: *I don't like the souvenirs. My luggage is too small. I don't have any money. Go away, leave me alone.*

They do not appreciate my words, how hard it was for me to learn them. They turn their backs in disgust. They like my husband. *Fernandez, sí. Liriano, sí.* This is the only Spanish he knows.

They give me their names at my window:
Jorge, Hugo and Jesus.
Their ages surprise me, too small for thirteen.

Jesus, the talker, sticks his hand out for money.
We need it for pencils, he shows me and writes
words on pink palm with brown fingers.
My sun-darkened hands turn up several coins,
I laugh to myself as they scramble.

Up the hill climbs another, limping like the wounded.
This is my brother, mi hermano, says Jesus.
He go school too, give him money?
This boy is different, something darker
than pain dulls his eyes.
Venga muchacho, I ask him to come, Jesus tells me
he can't speak or hear.

My fingers scratch for more change in my purse,
did deep into pockets, there is nothing.
That's okay lady, Jesus says and he turns,
hands his treasure over to his brother.
The boy hops forward a step, turns the coins in his hand,
then drags the leg back a safe distance.

When I am eighty-five
like my grandmother,
it will be the dogs I remember.

The city dogs, few that I saw,
were small, rat-nosed.
The kind you'd never let your children touch.
There are no words for their colours.

In the country, our tour bus drew stares
from women and children, working and playing
near bright blue painted shacks.
Then, to our right, fields of plantain,
to our left, one big dog,
skinned and hanging
beside a grass hut.
Lionel, our tour guide,
said it was a goat,
but I caught his smile to the driver.

Grandma smiles often now.
Her dry lips twist and curl,
her hands stroke the memories
of dogs: *Here King.*
             Here Lady.
             That's a good dog.

Just to stand at the edge   look forever

at this beauty   see nothing
                and everything
water is always
                my calling
I've known since a child   chasing waves
in a much colder sea

Ripples come first   wash my feet   tickle knees
higher   where blue coolness spreads

With whispers of mysteries   treasures untold
I plunge to the depths   and uncover
There is no one to witness
what is done in the deep
where Rattails and Black devils hunt
Even sunlight can no longer reach

At the centre of secrets
I allow it to enter
      here on the coral
      beneath in dark caves   the waves
break again and again

I did not choose this doll
for its beauty: uneven
red stitch of mouth,
nutbrown skin, lighter
than the woman's hands
who clothed it
in soiled lace.

This is not a doll
for Grandpa's knee girls;
would not sit properly
on dustfree shelves,
lifting its skirt,
pantyless.

I did not choose this doll
for beauty; I would not
place it in innocent arms.
A child at nightfall
clutching this doll
would toss in a sea
of blankets — trying, trying
to sleep.

I would not give this doll
to a child. I will never
build it a house with small beds,
a pretty kitchen. It should not
be here in my own.

Not far from the town
where I bought it,
people stick pins into
dolls like this.

This is a country I've captured
in pictures

Black girl dressed in white
selling peanuts
on the beach   Naked boy
drawing rivers in the sand
Pedro beside me   a ripe pineapple
between us

Man on the roadside   squatting
in the dust
Stretched leather skin
over bones

His is the picture
I did not have to take
Those white eyes
will follow me
everywhere

(A Found Poem, Saskatoon Star-Phoenix, 1987)

Maybe 150
no one can say for sure
difficult matching bodyparts
and it was dark, black
when the ocean claimed their boat
their freedom boat, six kilometres
off the northeast coast

An airforce pilot
actually saw the sharks
tearing apart the bodies

Back on land, another 150
waiting for freedom
were discovered, detained and questioned
to determine who was responsible
for planning the trip

i.

They spy our bus from the hills;
swarm like sharks to blood, these boys,
each begging to be my *secretario*
on the beach, the big beach -
Playa Grande.

I choose Pedro, he's loyal, like a lap dog he sits
just far enough away.
When the peddlers come, he advises:
        Larimar is a good price.
        They ask too much for the coral.
I buy blue stones for my friends.
A small black cross for my lover.

ii.

There is no time here, no awareness
of time, I mean.
The sun just gets higher, hotter and burns.
When I can't stand it,
the water is there, the waves
fold me backwards, throw me away,
then carry me back to the beach.

iii.

Here is peace. No sound but the waves,
No colour but blue, and Pedro.
I ask him to join me, sit on my towel.
Tell him there is another world.
        Do you want to go there, Pedro?
        Do you wonder what it's like?
He smiles at this, at all that he knows:
this place, the water, the sun.
His brown eyes give away nothing.

Tell him I am from Canada.
    No Pedro, not Toronto, Saskatchewan.
    There's no ocean, no mountains, there.
I reach for a stick and draw it for him,
a straight long line in the sand.
    Say it Pedro, Saskatchewan.
He tries. He fails.
Together we laugh at this word.

iv.

We sit like this for hours.
This is what I want to remember,
Pedro's warm skin so close to my own.

I cannot leave this boy on the beach,
I kiss him, run to my bus.
Pedro at my window, kissing my hand.
I give him the rest of my pesos.

Acknowledgements

Some of the poems in this book appeared in *Antigonish Review*, *Briarpatch*, *The Fiddlehead*, *Freelance*, *Grail*, *Grain*, *NeWest Review*, *Northward Journal*, *Other Voices*, *Poetry Canada Review*, and *Proem Canada*. A selection of "The Pedro Poems" was broadcast on CBC's "Ambience." The title poem, "A Few Words For January" won Honourable Mention in the 1989 Saskatchewan Writers Guild Literary Awards. Several poems in this collection comprised the manuscript which placed Runner-Up in the 1989 Kalamalka New Writers Competition.

The author thanks Lorna Crozier, Paddy O'Rourke, Glen Sorestad, members of the Saskatoon Writers' Bloc and others who provided invaluable editorial guidance.

On the occasion of this book's third printing, Shelley would like to thank Paula Patola, especially, and all the other teachers who enthusiastically support Saskatchewan writing in their classrooms. God bless you.

The author is grateful to the Saskatchewan Artists'/Writers' Colony Committee for providing an environment conducive to writing.

Special thanks to Troy, because he knows her best and loves her anyway.